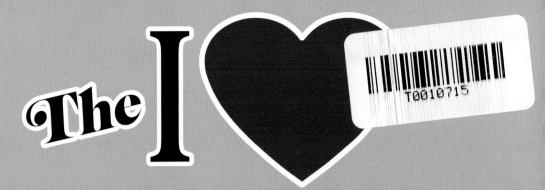

The I ♥ TRADER JOE'S® SNACK BOARDS COOKBOOK

50 Delicious Recipes for Charcuterie, Spreads, Platters, and More Using Ingredients from the World's Greatest Grocery Store

PAMELA ELLGEN

ULYSSES PRESS

Published by:
Ulysses Press
PO Box 3440
Berkeley, CA 94703
www.ulyssespress.com

ISBN: 978-1-64604-559-4
Library of Congress Control Number: 2023938311

Printed in China
10 9 8 7 6 5 4 3 2 1

Acquisitions editor: Kierra Sondereker
Managing editor: Claire Chun
Project editor: Paulina Maurovich
Editor: Phyllis Elving
Proofreader: Barbara Schultz
Cover artwork: from shutterstock.com—grapes and crackers © DiViArt; chips and pretzels © Natalya Levish; honey and Swiss cheese © overkoffeined; salami © Vector Tradition; cutting board © Sketch Master; utensil © chempina; background texture © N_A_T_A_L_I
Interior artwork: see page 126
Layout: what!design @ whatweb.com

To Jeremy and all our boys.

TABLE OF CONTENTS

Chapter **1**

Introduction

I'm so excited about this book! As someone who has been shopping at Trader Joe's for years, I consider it my go-to grocery store for unique and high-quality products.

In this book I'll be sharing my favorite Trader Joe's products and how to use them to create delicious and visually stunning charcuterie boards. And all the ingredients used in this book can be found at Trader Joe's, so you don't have to worry about making multiple grocery store trips.

But this book isn't just about Pinterest-worthy charcuterie—it's about making food more accessible and appetizing. From Italian antipasto platters to loaded cookie boards, I'll show you how to create boards that are not only delicious but also visually stunning.

If you're new to creating snack boards, don't worry! I've included tips on how to assemble a snack board, such as choosing the right board and arranging your ingredients. And most of the boards in this book take 10 minutes or less to prepare, perfect for busy weeknights or impromptu get-togethers.

So come along and join me in creating delicious and beautiful charcuterie boards with Trader Joe's products!

WHY TRADER JOE'S?

Trader Joe's offers unique and high-quality products that I can't find anywhere else, curated by a team of people I'm pretty sure I'd be friends with. Feels like having my own personal grocery concierge. Bougie.

The store also offers a lot of convenience foods that make cooking easy, especially after a long day at work. I'm especially fond of their refrigerated and frozen meals and sauces. I also love not having to worry about any unhealthy ingredients, such as MSG, trans fats, or artificial colors and flavors. They take health and well-being seriously.

The store has a friendly and laid-back atmosphere, making shopping there enjoyable (except on Sundays, seriously). That's by design. You feel like you're entering a cozy neighborhood grocery store.

And of course, their prices are very competitive, which is always a plus!

Finally, low-key healthy snacks and an affordable wine selection make this the perfect start to a tasty charcuterie board!

WHAT MAKES A CHARCUTERIE BOARD?

Once limited to just cheeses and meats, charcuterie boards now showcase a wide variety of ingredients organized around just about any theme or occasion.

Think Indian feast with basmati rice, chicken shawarma, madras lentils, warm garlic naan, and creamy yogurt sauce arranged on a butcher block and garnished with lemon, cucumber, and scallions.

Or a dessert board loaded with multicolored French macarons, dark chocolate ganache cake, raspberry shortbread cookies, and cocoa batons.

Creativity has its limits, though.

Portlandia, the sketch comedy television series starring Carrie Brownstein and Fred Armisen, features a hilarious segment called "We Can Pickle That!" In the opening scene, a farmer expresses his disappointment that his cucumbers haven't sold at the market, prompting Carrie and Fred to step in and declare "We can pickle that!" They go on to pickle eggs, and by the end of the sketch they're pickling broken high heels and CD jewel cases.

The same thing has happened with charcuterie, birthing an entire genre of chili con carne smeared across cutting boards, dining room tables laden with an excess of expensive appetizers, and every scrap of tile or slice of wood being transformed into a serving vessel. Nachos on a shovel, anyone?

When I crafted the board concepts for this book, I asked a few questions: Does this make the food easier to eat? Does it make it prettier? And does it make it more appetizing? I aimed for a combination of all three.

Above all, have fun! And enjoy the food!

ABOUT THE RECIPES AND INGREDIENTS

Most of the boards in this book take 10 minutes or less to prepare. And because this book is all about Trader Joe's, the ingredients can all be found at Trader Joe's—most of them year-round, though a handful are seasonal. Who really wants to go to multiple grocery stores? I write cookbooks for a living, and even I get tired of shopping. That said, you certainly can source many of the ingredients in this book from any store. Ingredients you can find anywhere are listed plainly (e.g., red onion, olive oil, etc.).

For recipes that call for specific Trader Joe's products, I include the full product name (e.g., Trader Joe's Organic Chunky Homestyle Guacamole). Even in these instances, substitutions may be needed if something is out of stock or you prefer an alternative. Unlike baking, which requires precision, creating snack boards invites creativity. Feel free to mix and match boards and swap out sauces, spreads, and other ingredients as you like.

Where appropriate, recipes are labeled "Vegan," "Vegetarian," or "Gluten-free." Also, where it's easy to omit or swap an ingredient, I've added the word "optional."

HOW TO ASSEMBLE A SNACK BOARD

You could arrange all the ingredients on your board in a haphazard way. That totally works! But if you want to create a work of art, here are a few tips to get you started:

CHOOSE THE RIGHT BOARD. Technically, anything that is flat, nonporous, and washable will work. I've opted for a handful of everyday cutting and serving boards—nothing too fancy, and nothing costing more than $30.

Select the correct size. You want everything to fit on the board without falling off or appearing sparse (unless that's the vibe you're looking for).

Consider the shape and texture of the food you'll be serving as you choose your board. Uncut cherry tomatoes were born to run. Either choose a platter with a slight rim, place them in a bowl, or take your chances and add them after the board has been placed in its serving location.

Consider the mood. Is it elegant or casual? Also think about color. If I'm serving lighter-colored ingredients, I prefer a darker board for contrast.

PLACE THE ANCHOR INGREDIENTS ON THE BOARD FIRST. Identify one or two primary ingredients, such as the waffles in the Waffles Board (page 21) or the cheese wedges in the Fruit and Cheese Dessert (page 103), and arrange those on the board. You want them to make a statement, to take up space, and to clearly show what the board is all about. Arrange the remaining ingredients around the anchor ingredients.

Personally, I avoid molding ingredients into fancy shapes. First, it screams 1980s, and not in a good way. Second, who really wants someone else warming up their prosciutto with their fingertips? But you do you.

PLACE SOME FOOD IN BOWLS. Place any sauces, wet foods (such as gherkins or olives), and small ingredients (such as almonds) in bowls. Don't worry about making sure the bowls all match. Just fit each ingredient to a bowl, choosing the smallest ones you can to avoid overwhelming the board. (And, of course, skip the dishes if you want to serve some things directly from the container they came in. No shame in that!) Place the bowls directly on the boards—staggered, in a pattern, or down the center.

FILL IN THE GAPS… OR DON'T. Finally, finish with garnishes such as fresh herbs or lemons, or save a handful of another ingredient on the platter to sprinkle over the board to fill in spaces. That said, don't fear the space between ingredients. Sometimes the prettiest boards have room to breathe, such as the Endless Summer board (page 44) or the Mixed Gyoza with Dipping Sauce (page 79).

HOW THE BOOK IS ORGANIZED

This book is organized into several recipe chapters. Chapter 2, Breakfast, is filled with scrumptious breakfast and brunch platters, many of which can be prepared the night before. From the vibrant Waffles Board (page 21) to the austere Post-Workout Protein Fix (page 25), there's a little something for everyone.

Chapter 3, Classic Charcuterie, has all the boards you've come to expect, from family-friendly cheese-and-cracker boards to Greek meze and Italian antipasto. It also has a couple of boards organized by theme and season, such as Festive Winter Board with Spiced Pecans, Pears, and Gorgonzola (page 35).

Chapter 4 has recipes that you can mix and match to make an Epic Tapas party. Each one could stand on its own with the addition of a baguette and a package of Trader Joe's Spanish Brand Deli Selection and Trader Joe's Spanish Cheese Tapas Sampler.

Chapter 5 includes simple snack boards with five ingredients or fewer. Yes, they're simple—that's the point. They're perfect for those times when you have guests coming over but dinner is at least an hour out. No need for anything fancy. My kids adore the recipes in this chapter—the Carolina Gold Wings with Ranch (page 64) and Latkes with Applesauce and Sour Cream (page 72) ranked in their top five in the whole book!

Chapter 6 has boards that stand in for a meal. In keeping with the board theme, they're pretty and have an experiential component, especially the Mongolian Barbecue (page 85) and Cheese Fondue (page 94). Chapter 7 is all about sweet things. From a Movie Night Board (page 99) to Fruit and Cheese Dessert (page 103), there's a little something for everyone. Finally, Chapter 8 has a handful of extras that you can add to any board—Pickled Vegetables, Spiced Nuts, Compound Butters, and Dipping Oils.

HOW TO GET GOOD PICTURES

Let's be real—part of the attraction of charcuterie boards is how pretty they are. So I'm guessing you'll want to snap a picture of your completed board.

I've been doing food photography for the better part of a decade, but I'll let you in on a little secret—I shot every recipe in this book with my iPhone. Yup, you read that right. That means you can capture your own gorgeous boards without a fancy camera setup. Here are a few tricks you can use to get perfect pictures every time. Make sure to tag me @surfgirleats on Instagram and share your food pics with the hashtag #tjsnackboard.

STYLE THE FOOD. This doesn't mean carving radishes into swans. It does mean creating patterns and contrast, garnishing with fresh herbs and other edibles, and making sure to clean up unintentional splatters. Create alternating rows of chips going one way and cheese going another way. Stack some food in mounds. Don't be afraid to elevate some of the food.

ENSURE BOTH AMBIENT AND DIRECTIONAL LIGHT. Daylight is best (not overhead lights), so it's easiest if you prep and shoot before the sun goes down. Also, I like strong directional light (i.e., coming from one side). The ambient light ensures that you see the detail and color in the food. The directional light makes it interesting. I love a gentle backlight, too.

PHOTOGRAPH FROM OVERHEAD. This is a tip I learned from a friend who's a magazine food stylist, and I've used it ever since. The other option is to shoot at eye level with the food, or at a 45-degree angle. When you're shooting things that have straight lines, such as boards, make sure they line up (editing works to fix this to some extent, but it's more difficult than you might think).

USE PORTRAIT MODE. Use portrait mode and adjust the depth of field (on an iPhone, adjusting the depth of field is done with the button that looks like a cursive *f* with a circle around it). The shallowest depth of field is 1.4, which makes only a small plane of the subject in focus so that you can choose what to focus on. On iPhone, you can also adjust the depth of field when editing *after* shooting, amazingly enough.

CHOOSE YOUR BACKGROUND. Sometimes I set my board on the counter, the kitchen table, or even the floor if that provides better lighting and contrast. I also like scattering some of the ingredients around the board haphazardly. No, I wouldn't serve it that way, but it gives the picture an unstudied look, ironically.

Chapter 2

Breakfast

FRUIT BOARD

Enjoy this fruit board as breakfast, an afternoon snack, or a healthy dessert. Of course, you can mix and match the fruit according to what looks good at your Trader Joe's and purchase whole fruit (such as watermelon) instead of packages. The Greek yogurt makes a lovely dip or can be drizzled over fruit on individual serving plates.

1 (6-ounce) container Trader Joe's Greek Nonfat Plain Yogurt

1 lemon, zest and juice

1 tablespoon Trader Joe's 100% Pure Maple Syrup or honey

1 (6-ounce) container raspberries

1 bunch green grapes

1 (16-ounce) container strawberries

1 (6-ounce) container blackberries

2 oranges, unpeeled, sliced in rounds

4 fresh mint sprigs or citrus leaves

VEGETARIAN, GLUTEN-FREE

In a small bowl, combine the yogurt with the zest and 1 teaspoon juice from the lemon, along with the maple syrup or honey. Place on your serving board or platter.

Arrange the fruit on the board, alternating colors and textures. Garnish with the fresh mint or citrus leaves.

Serve at once, or cover loosely with plastic wrap and refrigerate for up to 4 hours.

SERVES: 4 to 6
PREP TIME: 10 minutes

EURO BREAKFAST

I lived in England for about a year and adored the continental breakfasts I had while traveling by train through Europe, especially Germany.

1 (16-ounce) bag Trader Joe's Just the Clusters Vanilla Almond Granola Cereal

1 (32-ounce) container Trader Joe's Greek Nonfat Plain Yogurt

1 (9.3-ounce) package Trader Joe's Cage Free Fresh Hard-Cooked Peeled Eggs, halved or left whole

1 (6-ounce) container raspberries

1 (6-ounce) container blackberries

1 (8-ounce) package Trader Joe's Uncured Black Forest Ham

Place the granola and Greek yogurt in separate bowls and set them on your board or platter.

Arrange the remaining ingredients around the bowls to serve.

SERVES: 4
PREP TIME: 10 minutes

OATMEAL BOARD

Everyone likes their oatmeal a different way—at least my boys do. One likes raisins. The other likes blueberries. As for me, caramelized bananas hit the spot. This board offers oatmeal to please everyone.

2 cups Trader Joe's Rolled Oats

6 cups water

sea salt

1 tablespoon butter, plus more for serving

2 bananas, sliced

2 tablespoons Trader Joe's Organic Brown Sugar, plus more for serving

½ cup Trader Joe's Organic Unsweetened Coconut Chips

1 cup fresh blueberries

1 cup strawberries, sliced

½ cup Trader Joe's Organic Thompson Seedless Raisins

½ cup granola of choice

¼ cup Trader Joe's Unsalted Dry Toasted Silvered Almonds

VEGETARIAN

Place the oats, water, and a pinch of sea salt in a medium saucepan and bring to a simmer over high heat. Reduce the heat to low, cover, and cook for 3 more minutes. Turn off the heat and allow to rest while you prepare the rest of the ingredients.

Melt 1 tablespoon butter in a large skillet over medium-high heat. Gently dust the banana slices with the 2 tablespoons brown sugar, then sear on both sides until caramelized, about 2 minutes per side. Transfer the banana slices to a bowl and set on the serving board.

Place the coconut chips, blueberries, strawberries, raisins, granola, and almonds in separate small bowls and set on the board along with additional butter and brown sugar for serving. Divide the oatmeal into individual serving bowls and enjoy it hot.

SERVES: 4
PREP TIME: 10 minutes
COOK TIME: 10 minutes

WAFFLES BOARD

I love waffles. But let's be honest—if you're serving more than one or two people, you're going to end up in the kitchen cooking waffle after waffle and never getting to enjoy the meal with your family. TJ's frozen Belgian Waffles make it easy to serve waffles for a crowd without spending all morning in the kitchen.

1 pint raspberries

1 pound strawberries

2 bananas, sliced

2 oranges, sliced

1 (13-ounce) jar Trader Joe's Cocoa Almond Spread

1 cup Trader Joe's 72% Cacao Dark Chocolate Chips

1 cup Trader Joe's 100% Pure Maple Syrup

1 stick butter, at room temperature

2 packages Trader Joe's Authentic Belgian Waffles

VEGETARIAN

Arrange the raspberries, strawberries, and banana and orange slices on a board or platter, leaving a large section down the middle of the board for the waffles.

Place the cocoa almond spread and the chocolate chips in separate bowls, and pour the maple syrup into a small carafe. Place on the board along with the butter.

Just before serving, cook the waffles according to the package instructions. Arrange them on the board and serve immediately.

SERVES: 4
PREP TIME: 10 minutes
COOK TIME: 5 minutes

AVOCADO TOASTS

I'm a millennial. Barely. Maybe that's why I have very high standards for avocado toast. I snagged this recipe from a chef at one of my favorite spots in Santa Barbara. Avocado toasts are best enjoyed fresh—the moment you spread the avocado on the bread, the clock starts ticking. This board lets guests build their own toast when they're ready to enjoy it.

4 avocados

2 tablespoons extra-virgin olive oil, divided

1 teaspoon + 1 tablespoon lemon juice, divided

sea salt

2 tablespoons Trader Joe's Organic Tahini

1 to 2 tablespoons water

1 (16-ounce) container Trader Joe's Mini Heirloom Tomatoes

1 (2-ounce) container Trader Joe's Organic Micro Greens

1 tablespoon balsamic vinegar (optional), for drizzling over the toasts

1 (2.3-ounce) jar Trader Joe's Everything but the Bagel Sesame Seasoning Blend

1 Trader Joe's Stone Hearth Baked French Loaf

VEGAN

Halve the avocados and scoop the flesh into a medium bowl. Add 1 tablespoon olive oil and 1 teaspoon lemon juice and use a fork to mash. Season to taste with salt. Set the bowl on a serving board or platter.

In a separate bowl, whisk the remaining 1 tablespoon olive oil and 1 tablespoon lemon juice with the tahini. Thin with 1 to 2 tablespoons water until it's the right consistency to drizzle. Season to taste with salt and place on the serving board.

Arrange the tomatoes, microgreens, and seasoning blend on the board.

Toast 4 slices of the French bread and add them to the board. Serve immediately.

SERVES: 4
PREP TIME: 15 minutes

POST-WORKOUT PROTEIN FIX

I love lifting weights and then having my morning protein shake. But sometimes I want a more substantial post-workout meal. What this board lacks in glamor, it makes up for in function. It pairs high-protein hard-boiled egg and Greek yogurt with complex and simple carbs, which helps post-workout recovery.

1 (7-ounce) container Trader Joe's Ruby Red Grapefruit Segments

1 Trader Joe's Cage-Free Fresh Hard-Cooked Peeled Egg, halved

1 (6-ounce) container Trader Joe's Greek Nonfat Plain Yogurt

1 slice bread of choice, toasted

1 tablespoon Trader Joe's Organic Almond Butter

VEGETARIAN

Arrange the grapefruit, egg halves, and yogurt container on a plate or small board.

Toast the bread and top it with the almond butter.

SERVES: 1
PREP TIME: 5 minutes

SMOKED SALMON AND BAGELS BOARD

The beauty of this classic brunch combo belies its simplicity. Just remove the ingredients from the packages, place on the board, and serve. My youngest son, Cole, helped me style this board and asked excitedly, "So, people are going to see the cucumbers I arranged?" Yes, they are!

1 (8-ounce) package cream cheese

2 tablespoons capers (optional)

1 package plain bagels

4 Persian cucumbers, sliced

1 (8-ounce) package Trader Joe's Nova Salmon Pieces

1 lemon, sliced

fresh herbs, such as parsley and dill, for garnish

1 (2.3-ounce) jar Trader Joe's Everything but the Bagel Sesame Seasoning Blend

Place the cream cheese and capers, if using, into individual serving bowls and place them on the board. Arrange the bagels, cucumbers, salmon, and lemon slices around the bowls and garnish with fresh herbs. Set the seasoning blend on the board or on the side.

Toast each bagel individually if desired.

SERVES: 4
PREP TIME: 10 minutes

Chapter 3

Classic Charcuterie

KID-FRIENDLY CHEESE AND CRACKERS

I created this board for my boyfriend, Jeremy, and our kids—we have five boys between us—to enjoy while we built gingerbread houses. It was important to me to have cheeses and meats that everyone would enjoy. Smoked salami and colby jack were perfect. I also opted for kid-friendly vegetables—cucumbers and carrots.

1 (12.35-ounce) jar Trader Joe's Cornichons

1 (16-ounce) package Trader Joe's Organic Carrots of Many Colors, Cut & Peeled

1 (16.4-ounce) package Trader Joe's Scalloped Cracker Trio

1 (4-ounce) package Trader Joe's Uncured Applewood Smoked Salami

1 (12-ounce) package Trader Joe's Sliced Colby Jack Cheese

1 (16-ounce) container Trader Joe's Persian Cucumbers

Place the cornichons and carrots in bowls and set them on the board.

Arrange the remaining ingredients in patterns around the bowls, keeping the crackers separate from the cucumbers so the crackers won't get soggy.

SERVES: 4 to 6
PREP TIME: 5 minutes

CRUDITE RAINBOW

This board's gorgeous rainbow hues make it fun to serve during Pride Month. Feel free to swap out specific vegetables for ones you prefer, ideally choosing something of the same color. When it comes to dipping sauces, the sky's the limit. I love Trader Joe's Sour Cream Spinach dip or Trader Joe's Mediterranean Creamy and Smooth Hummus.

8 ounces Trader Joe's Haricot Verts

1 (8-ounce) package Trader Joe's Steamed & Peeled Baby Beets, drained and quartered

1 (16-ounce) package Trader Joe's Les Petites Carrots of Many Colors

1 red bell pepper, sliced

1 (16-ounce) package Trader Joe's Mini Heirloom Tomatoes

1 orange bell pepper, sliced

1 yellow bell pepper, sliced

1 cucumber, sliced

fresh parsley and dill (optional)

VEGAN, GLUTEN-FREE

Bring a large pot of heavily salted water to a boil over high heat. Then add the green beans and cook for 3 minutes, or until they are bright green. Drain under cold running water until the beans are no longer warm to the touch (or plunge them into a bowl of ice water).

Arrange the ingredients on your board, starting with the beets and purple carrots on one end, moving on to red bell pepper slices and red tomatoes, carrots and orange bell pepper slices, yellow bell pepper slices and yellow tomatoes, and finally the green beans and cucumber slices.

Garnish with fresh parsley and dill, if using, and serve with Essential Dip (page 123).

SERVES: 4
PREP TIME: 15 minutes
COOK TIME: 3 minutes

FESTIVE WINTER BOARD WITH SPICED PECANS, PEARS, AND GORGONZOLA

The contrast of flavors on this board keeps you coming back for bite after bite. Spicy pecans, sweet pears and grapes, salty meats, and tangy gorgonzola are perfect together. I often serve soup on Christmas Eve, so adding this board as a hearty appetizer ensures that everyone gets enough to eat.

1 (5-ounce) bag Trader Joe's Sweet and Spicy Pecans or 1 cup Spiced Nuts (page 115)

1 (4-ounce) wedge Trader Joe's Crumbly Gorgonzola Cheese

1 (20-ounce) container Trader Joe's Red Seedless Grapes

1 (16-ounce) package Trader Joe's Persian Cucumbers, quartered lengthwise

2 pears, red and green

1 (6-ounce) package Trader Joe's Spanish Brand Deli Selection

GLUTEN-FREE

Place the pecans in a bowl and set on the serving board.

Add the gorgonzola and then arrange the remaining ingredients artfully around the board, keeping the fruit away from the cheese to avoid dampening it.

SERVES: 4
PREP TIME: 10 minutes

MARCELLA'S BABY SHOWER BOARD

This board began as the centerpiece for my best friend's baby shower. My favorite cheeses, meats, fruit, and spreads from TJ's overflowed any clever theme I had in mind, not to mention the largest cutting board at her mom's house! On the plus side, it satisfied every palate. Use your largest board or even a baking sheet to serve this array.

1 (6-ounce) package Trader Joe's Roasted & Salted Marcona Almonds with Rosemary

1 (11-ounce) package Trader Joe's Sour Cream Spinach Dip

1 (12.35-ounce) jar Trader Joe's Cornichons

1 wedge Trader Joe's Saint André Triple Crème Brie

1 (7-ounce) wedge Trader Joe's Unexpected Cheddar Cheese

1 (4-ounce) package Trader Joe's Uncured Applewood Smoked Salami

1 (32-ounce) container of grapes

1 container blackberries

1 (16-ounce) package Trader Joe's Les Petites Carrots of Many Colors

1 Trader Joe's Organic French Baguette, sliced

Place the almonds, spinach dip, and cornichons in separate bowls and set on the serving board. Add the brie and cheddar cheeses.

Arrange the remaining ingredients around the board to give it an abundant, overflowing feel.

SERVES: 4
PREP TIME: 10 minutes

ITALIAN ANTIPASTO

The most literal translation of antipasto is "before the meal." So for this board I opt for a handful of piquant ingredients—things you'll want to nibble on but not make a full meal of. This spread is designed to sharpen your appetite, not dull it with a lot of crackers, bread, and filler ingredients.

1 (8-ounce) container Trader Joe's Ciliegine Whole Milk Fresh Mozzarella

1 (11.64-ounce) jar Trader Joe's Grilled Pitted Chalkidiki Variety Green Olives in Oil

1 (10.23-ounce) jar Trader Joe's Sweet Picanté Peppers

1 (5-ounce) package Trader Joe's Columbus Calabrese Salame

1 (4-ounce) package Trader Joe's Sliced Prosciutto

1 (4-ounce) wedge Trader Joe's Crumbly Gorgonzola Cheese

Trader Joe's Marinated Artichokes (optional)

Marinated sun-dried tomatoes (optional)

1 cup Trader Joe's Mini Heirloom Tomatoes

fresh herbs such as oregano, basil, or parsley, for garnish

GLUTEN-FREE

Place the mozzarella, olives, and peppers in individual serving bowls and set them on the board.

Arrange the salame, prosciutto, and gorgonzola around the bowls. Add the artichokes and sun-dried tomatoes, if using. Scatter the tomatoes and herbs around the board to fill in the blank spaces.

SERVES: 6 to 8
PREP TIME: 10 minutes

MARIA'S GREEK MEZE PLATTER

My dad's wife, Maria, was born on a tiny island in Greece and was adopted by an American couple as a very young child. While she effuses classic Greek warmth and personality, she eschews some quintessential Greek foods—feta, tomatoes, and olives. So this board skips these predictable ingredients while still capturing the essence of a sun-drenched summer on a Greek island. Be sure to check the note at the end of the recipe for several delicious optional add-ins, all from Trader Joe's.

1 (16-ounce) package boneless, skinless chicken thighs, cut into 2-inch pieces

4 cloves garlic, minced

2 tablespoons minced fresh oregano (or 2 teaspoons dried)

1 tablespoon minced fresh rosemary (or 1 teaspoon dried)

zest and juice from 1 lemon

¼ cup extra-virgin olive oil

1 teaspoon sea salt

½ teaspoon freshly ground black pepper

1 (5-ounce) package Trader Joe's Chevre Creamy, Fresh Goat Cheese

1 (4-ounce) package Trader Joe's Sliced Prosciutto

12 Trader Joe's Organic Pitted Medjool Dates

1 mini watermelon, cut into 1-inch pieces

1 (9.8-ounce) can Trader Joe's Greek Chickpeas with Parsley & Cumin

1 (18-ounce) package Trader Joe's Pita Bread

4 Persian cucumbers, quartered lengthwise

fresh herbs such as mint and oregano, for garnish

VEGETARIAN, GLUTEN-FREE

Place the chicken in a glass dish and add the garlic, oregano, rosemary, lemon zest and juice, olive oil, salt, and pepper. Set aside to marinate at room temperature for 30 minutes, or refrigerated for up to 8 hours. Thread the chicken onto wooden skewers.

While the chicken marinates, cut the goat cheese into 8 pieces. Wrap each one in a slice of prosciutto, covering all sides of the cheese. Thread the little packages onto two wooden skewers.

Preheat a gas or charcoal grill to medium high. Cook the chicken, turning frequently until it is cooked through to an internal temperature of 165°F. Cook the goat cheese parcels for about 5 minutes total, until the prosciutto is beginning to crisp and the centers are just warmed through.

Place the watermelon and chickpeas into separate bowls and set them on the board. Arrange the cooked chicken skewers on the board. Remove the goat cheese parcels from the skewers and place them on the board with the dates. Add the cucumber and pita and garnish with herbs.

SERVES: 4 to 6
PREP TIME: 10 minutes, plus 30 minutes for marinating the chicken
COOK TIME: 15 minutes

• •

Optional add-ins: Trader Joe's Tzatziki Creamy Garlic Cucumber Dip, Trader Joe's Dolmas Vine Leaves Stuffed with Rice, Trader Joe's Authentic Greek Feta, Trader Joe's Grilled Pitted Chalkidiki Variety Green Olives in Oil, Trader Joe's Greek Spanakopita.

• •

MIDDLE EASTERN MEZE

There's a neighborhood restaurant near my house called Shak's. While their hummus is unbeatable, their hours are sometimes a little tricky to figure out. This board holds me over when Shak's is closed. It's filling enough that it could easily stand in for a full meal.

1 (12-ounce) package Trader Joe's frozen Fully Cooked Falafel

1 (16-ounce) container hummus

1 (12-ounce) jar olives, such as Castelvetrano, Chalkidiki, or Kalamata

4 Trader Joe's Persian Cucumbers, sliced

1 (16-ounce) package Trader Joe's Mini Heirloom Tomatoes

VEGAN

Prepare the falafel according to the package instructions, preheating the oven to 325°F and spreading the falafel on a rimmed baking sheet. Bake for 10 to 15 minutes, or until heated through and crisp.

While the falafel heats, place the hummus and olives in bowls and set them on the board. Set a large bowl on the board for the falafel. Arrange the cucumbers and tomatoes around the bowls.

When the falafel is cooked, transfer it to the bowl on the board. Serve warm.

SERVES: 4
PREP TIME: 10 minutes
COOK TIME: 10 to 15 minutes

ENDLESS SUMMER

The Shore Room is an indoor-outdoor bar overlooking the ocean in southern California at Oceanside Pier, my favorite surf spot. Jeremy and I love winding down on a Friday night with a glass of wine and their charcuterie board. It's simple, beautiful, and effortless—like a warm summer evening.

Pickled Vegetables (page 112), drained

1 (6-ounce) package Trader Joe's Gourmet Deli Selection, with Calabrese Salame, Del Duca Prosciutto, and Capocollo

2 tablespoons Trader Joe's Seville Orange Marmalade

1 piece honeycomb from Trader Joe's Honey with Honeycomb, Grade A Honey

¼ cup Trader Joe's Dried Fruit Golden Berry Blend

1 wedge Trader Joe's Truffle Pecorino cheese, cut into pieces

1 wedge Trader Joe's Saint André Triple Crème Brie cheese, sliced

1 wedge Trader Joe's Comté cheese, sliced

¼ cup assorted olives, drained

¼ cup assorted nuts, such as walnuts, almonds, and macadamia nuts

GLUTEN-FREE

Arrange the ingredients casually on a large board. None of them have to be in a bowl.

SERVES: 2 to 4
PREP TIME: 10 minutes

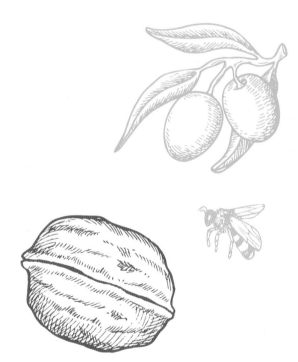

Chapter 4

Epic Tapas

BAKED FETA

I love the contrasting flavors of the honey, tangy feta, and herbaceous oregano and thyme. Be careful not to overcook this dish—the feta will get firm and crumbly and the honey will burn if heated too long. The goal is to make it warm and sweet, not to actually cook it.

2 tablespoons olive oil

1 (8-ounce) block Trader Joe's Feta Cheese

4 fresh oregano sprigs

4 fresh thyme sprigs

2 tablespoons Trader Joe's Honey with Honeycomb, Grade A Honey

freshly ground black pepper

bread of choice for serving

VEGETARIAN, GLUTEN-FREE

Preheat the oven to 375°F.

Place the olive oil and the feta in a small baking dish or a cast-iron skillet. Add the fresh oregano and thyme leaves, spreading them out evenly over the feta.

Drizzle the honey on the feta, then sprinkle freshly ground black pepper over the top.

Bake for 10 to 15 minutes, until the cheese is soft and gooey and the honey has started to caramelize on top. Remove from the oven and let cool for a few minutes before serving.

SERVES: 4
PREP TIME: 10 minutes
COOK TIME: 10 to 15 minutes

ROASTED BRUSSELS SPROUTS

Just about every appetizer menu for the past decade has offered some version of roasted Brussels sprouts. This is my go-to recipe. For a vegetarian version, I skip the bacon and opt for dried cherries, gorgonzola cheese, and finely chopped toasted pecans.

2 slices Trader Joe's Uncured Applewood Smoked Bacon, cut in ½-inch pieces

2 tablespoons olive oil

1 pound Brussels sprouts, trimmed and halved

3 cloves garlic, minced

salt and freshly ground black pepper

1 tablespoon good-quality balsamic vinegar

¼ cup Trader Joe's Grated Parmesan Cheese

GLUTEN-FREE

Preheat the oven to 400°F.

In a large, oven-safe skillet (such as cast-iron), cook the bacon pieces on the stovetop over medium-low heat until cooked through, about 10 minutes. Use a slotted spoon to transfer the pieces to a paper towel.

In a large bowl, combine the olive oil, Brussels sprouts, and minced garlic. Toss until the Brussels sprouts are well coated.

Spread the Brussels sprouts out in a single layer in the skillet and season to taste with salt and freshly ground pepper. Roast in the preheated oven for 20 minutes, or until tender and golden brown.

Remove the Brussels sprouts from the oven and drizzle with the balsamic vinegar. Transfer to a serving dish and sprinkle the cooked bacon and the parmesan cheese over the top.

SERVES: 4
PREP TIME: 10 minutes
COOK TIME: 30 minutes

BACON-WRAPPED DATES

These dates are full of surprises! The combination of sweet dates, salty bacon, creamy manchego cheese, and crunchy Marcona almonds creates a flavor explosion with every bite. This recipe is also incredibly easy to make, with just a few simple ingredients and minimal prep time.

20 Trader Joe's Organic Pitted Medjool Dates

4 ounces Trader Joe's Manchego Anejo Cheese, cut into small pieces

20 Trader Joe`s Roasted and Salted Marcona Almonds with Rosemary

10 slices bacon, cut in half crosswise

GLUTEN-FREE

Preheat the oven to 400°F. Line a baking sheet with parchment paper.

Stuff each date with a piece of manchego cheese and an almond, then close the date around the filling.

Wrap a half slice of bacon around each date.

Place the bacon-wrapped dates seam-side-down on the lined baking sheet. making sure they are spaced evenly. Bake for 15 to 20 minutes, or until the bacon is crisp and the dates have caramelized.

Remove from the oven and let cool for at least 5 minutes before serving.

SERVES: 4
PREP TIME: 10 minutes
COOK TIME: 15 to 20 minutes

ROASTED POTATOES WITH GOAT CHEESE AND HONEY

Jeremy and I enjoyed this tapa at a tiny restaurant on the North Shore of Oahu. The original version had cured Spanish chorizo, but because my local Trader Joe's doesn't carry that I've opted for another slightly spicy, cured sausage—pepperoni. Sounds weird, but it totally works.

1½ pounds Trader Joe's Dutch Yellow Baby Potatoes, halved

2 tablespoons olive oil

1 teaspoon smoked paprika

¼ teaspoon cayenne pepper

sea salt

freshly ground black pepper

2 ounces Trader Joe's Uncured Pepperoni, sliced

2 tablespoons Trader Joe's Honey with Honeycomb, Grade A Honey

4 ounces Trader Joe's Chevre Goat Cheese, crumbled

GLUTEN-FREE

Preheat the oven to 400°F. Line a rimmed baking sheet with parchment paper.

In a large bowl, toss the potatoes with the olive oil, paprika, cayenne pepper, and a generous pinch of salt and freshly ground black pepper. Toss until the potatoes are well coated.

Spread the potatoes out in a single layer on the baking sheet, then roast for 25 to 30 minutes, or until they are tender and golden brown.

Remove the potatoes from the oven and add the pepperoni. Toss gently to mix and warm the pepperoni, then transfer to a serving dish.

Drizzle the honey and sprinkle the goat cheese over the top of the potatoes. Serve hot.

SERVES: 4
PREP TIME: 10 minutes
COOK TIME: 25 to 30 minutes

SPANISH TORTILLA WITH CALABRIAN CHILES AND GREMOLATA

While slightly more involved than most recipes in this book, this is definitely one you'll want to add to your tapas playbook. In Spain this tortilla—or Spanish omelet—is served at room temperature, often the day after it's been cooked. That works well for entertaining, because it's nice not to have to worry about everything being done at the same time!

4 medium Yukon Gold potatoes

1 medium onion

¼ cup olive oil

6 large eggs

salt and pepper

1 lemon

½ teaspoon coarse sea salt

½ bunch fresh parsley

1 clove garlic, smashed

1 (6.7-ounce) jar Trader Joe's Italian Bomba Hot Pepper Sauce

VEGETARIAN, GLUTEN-FREE

Peel and thinly slice the potatoes and onion.

Heat the olive oil in a 12-inch cast-iron skillet over medium heat. Add the potato and onion slices, stirring to coat them with the oil. Cook for about 20 to 25 minutes, stirring occasionally, until the potatoes are tender and lightly browned.

In a mixing bowl, beat the eggs and season with salt (reserve the coarse salt for the gremolata) and pepper.

Pour this mixture into the skillet, spreading it evenly. Cook over medium heat for 5 to 7 minutes, or until the edges are set and the top is still slightly runny. While it cooks, preheat the oven to 375°F.

Transfer the skillet to the heated oven. Bake for about 10 minutes, or until the mixture is fully cooked and the top is golden brown.

While the tortilla bakes, make the gremolata. Remove two 3-inch strips of lemon peel, avoiding the white pith as much as possible. Place the coarse sea salt, parsley, garlic, and lemon peels on a cutting board. Using a chef's knife, chop all the ingredients until finely minced. Place in a small bowl.

Remove the skillet from the oven and let cool for a few minutes. Use a spatula to loosen the edges of the tortilla. Place a large plate on top and invert the skillet to release the tortilla onto the plate. Alternately, you can serve directly from the skillet.

Cut into wedges and serve warm or at room temperature along with the gremolata and chili pepper sauce.

SERVES: 4
PREP TIME: 10 minutes
COOK TIME: 40 minutes

SPICY SPANISH GARLIC SHRIMP WITH GARLIC TOASTS

Garlic shrimp is a classic Spanish tapa that can be found in many restaurants and bars. This dish is known as gambas al ajillo in Spanish, and it has a bold, savory flavor that is super garlicky and slightly smoky. A quarter cup of olive oil may seem like a lot, but the toast does a great job of sopping it up.

¼ cup + 1 tablespoon olive oil, divided

6 minced cloves garlic + 1 halved clove garlic, divided

1 teaspoon smoked paprika

pinch red chili flakes

½ teaspoon sea salt

freshly ground black pepper

1 pound jumbo shrimp, peeled and deveined

8 slices Trader Joe's Organic French Baguette, or gluten-free bread

1 tablespoon red wine vinegar

1 tablespoon minced fresh parsley

GLUTEN-FREE OPTION

In a medium bowl, combine the ¼ cup olive oil, 6 minced cloves garlic, smoked paprika, chili flakes, salt, and pepper to taste. Add the shrimp and toss gently to coat. Let marinate at room temperature for at least 30 minutes, or cover and refrigerate for up to 2 hours.

While the shrimp marinates, preheat the oven to 350°F and make the garlic toast. Rub the slices of bread with the halved garlic and brush lightly with the 1 tablespoon olive oil.

Bake the bread slices for about 5 to 7 minutes, or until golden brown and crisp. Set aside.

Heat a large skillet over medium-high heat. Add the marinated shrimp, scraping any remaining marinade from the bowl into the pan. Sear for 1 to 2 minutes, turning once or twice, until the shrimp are just barely cooked through. Season with the red wine vinegar and parsley. Transfer to a serving bowl and serve with the garlic toasts.

SERVES: 4
PREP TIME: 10 minutes
COOK TIME: 1 to 2 minutes

Chapter 5

Five-Ingredients-or-Fewer Snack Boards

MEDITERRANEAN HUMMUS AND VEGGIES

Trader Joe's Mediterranean hummus is the best I've ever tasted. Pair it with crisp Persian cucumbers, sweet bell peppers, and carrots—or whatever vegetables you like best.

1 (16-ounce) container Trader Joe's Mediterranean Style Hummus Creamy & Smooth

2 yellow, red, or orange bell peppers, sliced

1 (16-ounce) package Trader Joe's Les Petites Carrots of Many Colors

4 Trader Joe's Persian Cucumbers, sliced crosswise

VEGETARIAN, GLUTEN-FREE

Place the hummus container on the serving board.

Arrange the vegetables around the hummus. That's it—you're ready to serve!

SERVES: 4
PREP TIME: 10 minutes

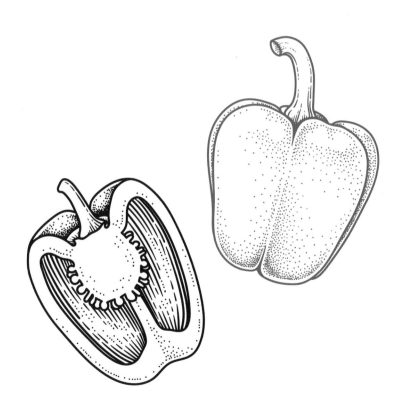

CAROLINA GOLD WINGS WITH RANCH

Carolina Gold Barbecue Sauce pleases everyone. It's sweet, sticky, and not too spicy. Pair it with a cool and creamy blue cheese dip or ranch dressing for serving the chicken wings.

2 pounds chicken wings

1 tablespoon canola oil

sea salt

freshly ground black pepper

1 bottle Trader Joe's Carolina Gold Barbecue Sauce

½ cup Trader Joe's Organic Ranch Dressing

8 celery spears, halved crosswise (to make 2 shorter pieces)

GLUTEN-FREE

Preheat the oven to 400°F. Dry the chicken wings thoroughly with paper towels, then toss them in a bowl with the oil. Season with salt and pepper.

Line a rimmed baking sheet with parchment paper. Place the wings on the lined sheet and bake for 45 minutes, turning once or twice or until cooked through and crisp. Remove from the oven and coat with the barbecue sauce. Return to the oven for 5 minutes to caramelize the sugars in the sauce, but be careful not to burn the wings.

Pour the dressing into a bowl and place on the serving board along with the celery. Add the cooked chicken wings and serve hot.

SERVES: 4
PREP TIME: 10 minutes
COOK TIME: 45 minutes

BUFFALO CHICKEN DIP WITH BLUE CHEESE AND CELERY

This might be the easiest "recipe" in this whole book. Think of it as a savory, grown-up version of "ants on a log." I loved the childhood snack of celery topped with peanut butter and raisins—a strange combination when you think about it, but it works. In this combo, the dip is delightfully spicy, contrasting with the funkiness of the gorgonzola and the vegetal crunch of the celery.

1 (12-ounce) container Trader Joe's Buffalo Style Chicken Dip

1 (4-ounce) wedge Trader Joe's Crumbly Gorgonzola Cheese

8 celery spears, halved crosswise (to create 2 shorter pieces)

GLUTEN-FREE

Arrange the chilled dip, cheese wedge, and celery spears on a serving board. You're ready to serve!

SERVES: 4
PREP TIME: 5 minutes

AREPAS AND EMPANADAS WITH JALAPEÑO SAUCE

Arepas are like subtly sweet South American grilled cheese sandwiches. Both arepas and empanadas are street foods, easy to hold because the tasty fillings are ensconced in dough. Balance their richness with Trader Joe's tangy and spicy Jalapeño Sauce.

1 (13.96-ounce) package Trader Joe's Corn and Cheese Arepas

2 (7.75-ounce) packages Trader Joe's Chicken & Chimichurri Empanadas

1 (10-ounce) bottle Trader Joe's Jalapeño Sauce

Cook the arepas and empanadas according to the package instructions. For the baking option, which I prefer, preheat the oven to 375°F. Place both the arepas and the empanadas on a baking sheet and cook for 20 to 25 minutes (see note below).

Pour the jalapeño sauce into a bowl and set it on the board. Cut the cooked arepas in half and arrange them on the serving board along with the empanadas. Serve hot.

SERVES: 4
PREP TIME: 10 minutes
COOK TIME: 20 to 25 minutes

••

Note: The baking temperatures listed for the arepas and empanadas differ. I went with the higher temperature called for by the empanadas. Also, since the arepas require an additional 5 minutes of cooking time, it worked fine to cook everything simultaneously.

••

RADISHES WITH KALAMATA AIOLI

The rich, umami flavors of this aioli balance the crisp, almost bitter radish. Even people who don't normally love radishes love this dip. It's inspired by the restaurant Gjelina in Venice, California.

½ cup mayonnaise

6 Trader Joe's Jumbo Pitted Greek Kalamata Olives, minced

1 small clove garlic, minced

1 teaspoon lemon juice

1 tablespoon minced parsley

1 (12-ounce) package Trader Joe's Radishes of Many Colors, or 2 bunches radishes, trimmed

VEGETARIAN, GLUTEN-FREE

In a small bowl, whisk together the mayonnaise, olives, garlic, lemon juice, and parsley. Place the bowl on a small board or platter.

Cut the radishes in half lengthwise and arrange on the platter around the aioli bowl. Serve the dip either chilled or at room temperature.

SERVES: 4
PREP TIME: 10 minutes

LATKES WITH APPLESAUCE AND SOUR CREAM

Despite its simplicity, this recipe was Cole's favorite. Then again, fried potato pancakes dipped in applesauce and sour cream is comfort food at its finest.

1 tablespoon canola oil

1 (10.6-ounce) package Trader Joe's Traditional Latkes

1 cup unsweetened applesauce

1 cup sour cream

fresh dill, for garnish

VEGETARIAN

Prepare the latkes according to your preferred method. I recommend pan-frying. Heat a large skillet over medium heat, add the tablespoon of canola oil, and heat until the oil is hot. Pan-fry the latkes for 4 to 5 minutes on each side, or until hot and crisp. Let dry on a paper towel.

Arrange the latkes on the serving board. Pour the applesauce and sour cream into individual bowls alongside the latkes. Garnish the board with fresh dill and serve while the latkes are hot.

SERVES: 4
PREP TIME: 10 minutes
COOK TIME: 8 minutes

SMOKY DEVILED EGGS

My great-aunt served deviled eggs every Easter, on a triangular platter with indentations for cradling the eggs. I hadn't thought much about deviled eggs again until I tried them at Marcus Samuelsson's Red Rooster restaurant in Harlem last summer. They were a revelation. Now I see them in all the hipster restaurants in California. They're part of a larger trend toward fresh takes on mid-century foods—think meatloaf, mac 'n' cheese, and JELL-O salad. Whether you make these to be ironic or sincere, Trader Joe's makes it easy with their peeled, hard-cooked eggs. If you've never used smoked paprika, prepare to want to put it on everything!

1 (9.3-ounce) package Trader Joe's Cage Free Fresh Hard-Cooked Peeled Eggs

¼ cup mayonnaise

¼ teaspoon Dijon mustard

¼ teaspoon smoked paprika, plus more for garnish

3 celery spears, for garnish

VEGETARIAN, GLUTEN-FREE

Slice each of the eggs in half lengthwise. Carefully scoop out the yolks and place them in a food processor along with the mayonnaise, mustard, and paprika. Blend until very smooth. If you have a piping bag, use it to pipe filling into each of the cooked egg-white halves. If not, use a teaspoon to scoop in the filling.

Sprinkle paprika over each egg half. Set the deviled eggs on a small serving board or platter. Garnish the board with the celery spears.

SERVES: 4 to 6
PREP TIME: 10 minutes

SHRIMP COCKTAIL WITH CRACKERS

I once heard that you don't know someone's character until you've shared a bowl of peeled shrimp with them. Whether it's a test of character or not, I don't know, but at restaurants you get maybe five shrimp in a shrimp cocktail order. Why do they do this to people? Unlike shrimp cocktail at a restaurant, this won't test your relationships.

While cooked, frozen shrimp would certainly make this come together more quickly, the texture just isn't that great. I recommend spending the extra five minutes cooking the shrimp yourself.

1 bottle Mexican lager

4 cups water

1 (16-ounce) package Trader Joe's Uncooked Wild Blue Shrimp

1 (11-ounce) bottle Trader Joe's Seafood Cocktail Sauce

1 (4.4-ounce) package Trader Joe's Classic Original Water Crackers

Pour the beer into a 2-quart saucepan and then add the 4 cups of water. Bring to a gentle simmer. Add the shrimp and cook until they curl slightly, about 2 minutes. Don't overcook! Transfer the shrimp to a colander and rinse with cold water, or plunge them into an ice-water bath to stop the cooking process. Pat dry with paper towels.

To serve, pour the cocktail sauce into a bowl and place it on your serving board. Line the bowl with the shrimp, or place them in a separate bowl. Arrange the crackers on the board and serve.

SERVES: 4
PREP TIME: 10 minutes
COOK TIME: 2 minutes

Note: Trader Joe's used to call its Mexican lager "Trader José's." It's their answer to Corona.

MIXED GYOZA WITH DIPPING SAUCE

I was tempted to fill this board with fresh mint and cilantro, lime wedges, and a dish of sesame seeds. But I was drawn to the board's minimalism and simplicity, echoing the food's Asian origins, so I let it be. Trader Joe's has a few different options for gyoza, or Japanese potstickers/dumplings. I chose their shrimp and vegetable gyoza. Do as you like.

2 to 4 tablespoons cooking oil

1 (16-ounce) package Trader Joe's frozen Thai Shrimp Gyoza

1 (16-ounce) package Trader Joe's frozen Thai Vegetable Gyoza

1 (10-ounce) bottle Trader Joe's Gyoza Dipping Sauce

Cook the gyoza according to the package instructions. Pan-frying, steaming, and microwaving are all options; I recommend the pan-fry method.

Heat 2 tablespoons of oil in a large skillet over medium-high heat. Or to keep the gyoza types separated and to cook more at once, use separate pans and heat oil in both. Add the gyoza, flat side down, and cook for 4 minutes, or until the skin turns golden brown. Add a few tablespoons of water, cover, and cook for 5 to 6 more minutes, or until the dumplings are heated all the way through.

Place the gyoza in serving bowls and set on the serving board. Pour the dipping sauce into a separate bowl and add it to the board. Serve the gyoza hot.

SERVES: 6
PREP TIME: 10 minutes
COOK TIME: 10 minutes

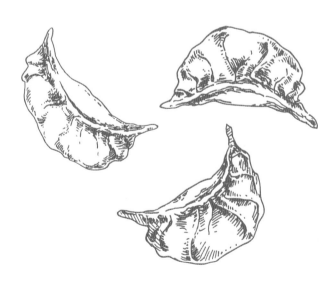

Chapter 6

Dinner

TACO AND TAQUITO PLATTER

The board has a way of elevating even frozen taquitos and tacos to a meal that feels festive. Here vegetarian black bean taquitos are paired with mini chicken tacos, guacamole, and salsa. To accompany them, I picked the Salsa Especial and Chunky Homestyle Guacamole—both of which are pretty mild in flavor—but you can choose whatever varieties you prefer.

1 (16-ounce) package Trader Joe's frozen Black Bean & Cheese Taquitos

1 (17.5-ounce) package Trader Joe's frozen Mini Chicken Tacos

1 (12-ounce) container Trader Joe's Salsa Especial

1 (10-ounce) container Trader Joe's Organic Chunky Homestyle Guacamole

1 (16-ounce) bag Trader Joe's Organic Blue Corn Tortilla Chips

cilantro sprigs for garnish (optional)

GLUTEN-FREE

Cook the taquitos and tacos according to the package instructions. The tacos take less time to cook, so place them in the oven at roughly the halfway mark for the taquitos.

Let the taquitos and tacos cool for 5 minutes and then transfer them to a serving board or platter. Pour the salsa and guacamole into individual small bowls and set them on the board.

Garnish the board with the corn tortilla chips and the cilantro, if using.

SERVES: 4
PREP TIME: 10 minutes
COOK TIME: 10 minutes

MONGOLIAN BARBECUE

For most dinners in our house, one of my kiddos is picking out the ingredient he doesn't like from his meal. With this board, as at Mongolian barbecue restaurants, everyone chooses exactly what they want. And because it's super easy, this is a great way for the kids to get involved in the cooking. The important thing here is not to add the noodles until the vegetables and meat are nearly cooked through, or they'll stick to the pan.

8 ounces spaghetti noodles

16 ounces Trader Joe's Shaved Beef Steak

1 (12.35-ounce) bottle Trader Joe's General Tsao Stir Fry Sauce

2 cups chopped broccoli florets

4 carrots, peeled and sliced

2 heads baby bok choy

canola oil

Cook the noodles al dente according to the package directions. Rinse under cool running water.

Place the noodles, beef, and stir-fry sauce in separate bowls and set them on the serving board. Arrange the fresh vegetables around them. Have each person assemble their own bowl of meat and vegetables (no sauce or noodles yet).

Heat a large wok or skillet over medium-high heat. When it's hot, add about 1 tablespoon canola oil. When it shimmers, add one of the assembled bowls and stir-fry for about 1 minute, or until the vegetables are brightly colored and the meat is nearly cooked.

Add a handful of noodles and a few tablespoons of sauce and stir-fry for another minute, until everything is heated through and the meat is no longer bright pink. Transfer to an individual serving bowl.

Repeat with the remaining portions. You may want to wipe out the skillet between bowls—or do as they do in restaurants and continue cooking every bowl without cleaning the wok in between.

SERVES: 4
PREP TIME: 15 minutes
COOK TIME: 15 minutes

HOT DOG BOARD

Originally I called this "hot dogs for a crowd," but because my two sons can polish off nearly the entire thing by themselves, I'm going with the less ambitious "board." Multiply this if you are feeding a crowd, and line up the hot dogs on a rimmed baking sheet. While hot dogs don't have quite the elegance of some other boards, I kind of like seeing them all lined up—it makes even ballpark food feel fancy! Do not do what some versions on Pinterest do and make mustard squiggles down the middle of every hot dog. Seriously, not everyone likes mustard. Especially kids.

2 (16-ounce) packages Trader Joe's All Natural Uncured Beef Hot Dogs

8 hot dog buns

¼ cup ketchup

¼ cup mustard

¼ cup pickle relish or minced gherkins

¼ cup thinly sliced red onion

Grill the hot dogs over medium-high heat for 10 minutes, until they're gently browned on all sides and heated through. During the last few minutes of cooking, toast the hot dog buns.

Place the condiments in small ramekins and line them up across the center of your board or platter.

Line the buns up on either side of the condiments and top with hot dogs. Serve immediately.

SERVES: 4
PREP TIME: 10 minutes
COOK TIME: 10 minutes

AMERICAN TACOS

Growing up, my family always had these tacos—made with flour tortillas, ground beef, shredded cheese, and iceberg lettuce. I was young enough, as I remember, to be upset when my taco fell apart. I now live in California, where tacos are more authentic to their Mexican origins—small corn tortillas topped with shredded meat and a smattering of diced onions and cilantro. Sure, there are many varieties, but none resemble the tacos of my childhood. So, in a fit of nostalgia, I put this board together.

1 tablespoon canola oil

2 tablespoons minced yellow onion

1 pound ground beef

1 tablespoon smoked paprika

1 teaspoon ground cumin

sea salt

freshly ground black pepper

1 cup shredded Mexican-style cheese blend

½ cup sour cream

½ cup diced tomatoes

¼ cup minced red onions

2 tablespoons tomato ketchup

1 (6-ounce) package crunchy corn tortilla shells

1 (16-ounce) package flour tortillas

2 cups shredded lettuce

1 avocado, sliced

Heat the oil in a large skillet over medium-high heat. Add the minced yellow onion and cook for 3 minutes, stirring occasionally until softened a bit. Add the ground beef, breaking it up with a wooden spoon. Add the paprika, cumin, and a generous pinch of salt and pepper. Cook until the meat begins to brown and none of it is pink. Remove from the heat. Season with salt and pepper to taste.

Place the ground beef in a bowl. (Or keep it hot by transferring it to a small cast-iron skillet that's been warmed.)

Place the cheese, sour cream, tomatoes, and minced red onion in small bowls and place on the board. Add the tortillas to the board and fit the lettuce and avocado into the remaining spaces. Serve immediately to let everyone assemble their own taco.

· ·

Note: Tacos originated in Mexico sometime before Spanish colonization. When the Spaniards arrived, they associated corn with native deities. But wheat flour was part of the Eucharist. Enter the flour tortilla. (Okay, I'm skipping a few years here.) Whether they connect one to God or not, I don't know, but they are softer.

· ·

SERVES: 4
PREP TIME: 10 minutes
COOK TIME: 13 minutes

PERSONAL PIZZAS

Trader Joe's Pizza Dough has been a staple in my kids' lives for as long as they can remember. Over the years, I've figured out how to coax the dough into the best version of itself. The key is to let it rest before baking and to cook on a lined baking sheet. Both may seem like a bit of a hassle, but why risk having a dense crust that's stuck to the pan? Here's a fun joke to share with your kids: Why did the hipster burn his mouth? Because he ate pizza before it was cool.

ESSENTIAL INGREDIENTS:

1 tablespoon olive oil

1 (16-ounce) package
Trader Joe's Pizza Dough,
plain or garlic and herb

1 jar marinara sauce

16 ounces (1⅓ packages)
Trader Joe's Shredded
Lite Mozzarella Cheese

TOPPING OPTIONS:

Trader Joe's Pesto alla Genovese

Trader Joe's Alfredo Pasta Sauce

Trader Joe's Organic Kansas
City Style BBQ Sauce

Trader Joe's Fresh Mozzarella
Cheese Log, sliced

Trader Joe's Uncured Pepperoni

Trader Joe's Uncured
Black Forest Ham

Trader Joe's Uncured
Applewood Smoked Salami

Trader Joe's Organic
Grilled Chicken Breast

bell pepper, diced

red onion, thinly sliced

fresh tomatoes, sliced

fresh pineapple, cut into chunks

cooked Italian sausage

black olives

mushrooms, sliced

fresh basil

red chili flakes

VEGETARIAN OPTION

Coat the interior of a small mixing bowl with the olive oil. Remove the pizza dough from the package and place it in the bowl, turning it once or twice to coat it in oil. Set in a warm place for an hour to rest (no need to cover), such as an oven prewarmed to about 100°F (but don't leave it on). This will make it infinitely easier to stretch.

Remove the dough from the oven if you placed it there. Heat the oven to 425°F. Line a large baking sheet with parchment paper.

Divide the dough into 4 equal portions and stretch each one into a circle, as thin as you can make it without ripping the dough. Place each dough circle on the lined baking sheet and bake for 7 minutes. (You can do this ahead of time. If you do it more than an hour ahead of time, seal the baked dough circles in a plastic bag until you are ready to add toppings and bake again.)

While the dough bakes, place the marinara sauce and cheese in bowls and set them on the board along with any additional toppings you've chosen. When the pizza crusts are ready, add them to the board as well.

Allow everyone to top their pizza as they like, then bake for an additional 8 to 10 minutes, or until the cheese is bubbling and beginning to brown. Allow to rest for 5 minutes before serving.

SERVES: 4
PREP TIME: 10 minutes, plus 1 hour for the dough to rest
COOK TIME: 15 minutes

INDIAN TAKEOUT

There's an amazing Indian takeout restaurant in Oceanside, California called Turmeric Hut. When Jeremy and I are craving Indian food, it's our go-to. On the rare occasions when we observe the financial unsustainability of getting takeout so often, we make "take-in." Trader Joe's makes it easy with several premade Indian side dishes that you can microwave right in the package. With freshly grilled shawarma chicken thighs and a spicy, creamy yogurt sauce, this board is about as close to takeout as you can get!

1 (18-ounce) package Trader Joe's Indian Style Flatbread, garlic or traditional

1 cup uncooked basmati rice

1½ cups water

sea salt

neutral oil, for brushing pan

1 (16-ounce) package Trader Joe's Shawarma Chicken Thighs

1 (5-ounce) container nonfat plain Greek yogurt

2 tablespoons extra-virgin olive oil, plus more for grilling chicken

1 clove garlic, minced

1 lemon, halved

1 (10-ounce) package Trader Joe's Indian Fare Kitchari

1 (10-ounce) package Trader Joe's Indian Fare Madras Lentils

2 Trader Joe's Persian Cucumbers, sliced

2 to 4 green onions for garnish

OPTIONAL ADD-ONS:
1 (10-ounce) package Trader Joe's Indian Fare Tikka Vegetables

1 package Trader Joe's frozen Mini Vegetable Samosas

1 (10-ounce) package Trader Joe's frozen Palak Paneer

VEGETARIAN OPTION, GLUTEN-FREE

Preheat the oven to 300°F. Wrap the flatbread in foil and place in the oven for 15 minutes to warm.

Bring the basmati rice, 1½ cups of water, and a generous pinch of sea salt to a simmer in a small pot over high heat. Reduce the heat to low, cover, and cook for 12 to 15 minutes, or until the rice has absorbed all the water and fluffs easily with a fork.

Heat a grill or a grill pan over medium-high heat and brush lightly with oil. Grill the chicken thighs for 5 to 6 minutes on each side, or until cooked through.

While the chicken and rice cook, whisk the yogurt with the olive oil, minced garlic, juice from half of the lemon, and a generous pinch of sea salt. Place in a small serving bowl and set on a large serving board.

Cook the kitchari and madras lentils in the microwave according to the package instructions, about 1 minute for each packet, or until hot. Alternately, place each in a small skillet and heat until barely simmering. Place in small serving bowls and set on the board.

Place the rice and chicken in separate serving bowls and arrange on the board. Add the flatbread, cucumbers, green onions, and remaining lemon half for garnish. Serve immediately.

SERVES: 4
PREP TIME: 10 minutes
COOK TIME: 15 minutes

CHEESE FONDUE

Steamed potatoes, vegetables, sausage, and bread—all dipped in gooey, melty cheese—makes a festive and filling dinner. Be sure to prep all the dipping ingredients before you prepare the cheese sauce so that it doesn't cool off before you can sit down to enjoy it. If you have a fondue pot and forks, use it! Otherwise, a cast-iron pot or even a glass bowl heated with boiling water will keep your cheese melty and warm.

FOR THE CHEESE SAUCE:

1 cup dry white wine, such as sauvignon blanc

1 clove garlic, minced

1 tablespoon lemon juice

¾ pound Trader Joe's Cheddar & Gruyere Mèlange Cheese, grated

¼ pound Trader Joe's Raw Milk Emmentaler Switzerland Cheese, grated

2 tablespoons cornstarch

1 teaspoon Dijon mustard

pinch ground nutmeg

FOR DIPPING:

1 to 2 cups cubed bread

1 (12-ounce) package chicken sausages, cooked and sliced

½ cup Trader Joe's Cornichons

1 cup lightly steamed broccoli florets

2 cups new potatoes, boiled (larger ones halved)

VEGETARIAN OPTION, GLUTEN-FREE OPTION

To make the cheese sauce, bring the wine, garlic, and lemon juice to a simmer in a small Dutch oven (such as Staub or Le Creuset) or other pot over medium-low heat.

In a small bowl, toss the grated cheeses with the cornstarch. Add the coated cheese a handful at a time to the wine, whisking after each addition, until it is all incorporated and the mixture is smooth. Stir in the mustard and nutmeg.

Remove the pan from the heat and place on a trivet in the center of the board. (Make sure not to set the pot directly on the board, to avoid scorching it.)

Arrange the bread cubes, sausage slices, cornichons, broccoli, and potatoes around the cheese sauce. Serve immediately.

SERVES: 4
PREP TIME: 10 minutes
COOK TIME: 10 minutes

Chapter 7

Desserts

MOVIE NIGHT BOARD

This is one of many boards in this book that is really a jumping off point for your own creativity—you can add or remove whatever you like! The key is to balance salty and sweet flavors. I recommend making the popcorn from scratch, because the texture and flavor are better when fresh. But do as you like—Trader Joe's offers popped popcorn.

⅓ cup popcorn kernels

2 tablespoons canola oil (if making on the stovetop)

3 tablespoons melted butter

sea salt

1 (8-ounce) package Trader Joe's Soft Strawberry Licorice Twists

1 (6-ounce) package Trader Joe's Bite-Sized Candy Coated Milk Chocolate Candies

1 (16-ounce) package Trader Joe's Dark Chocolate Peanut Butter Cups

1 (8-ounce) package Trader Joe's Dark Chocolate Covered Honey Grahams with Sea Salt

4 cups ridge-cut potato chips

VEGETARIAN

Cook the popcorn in a popcorn maker according to the manufacturer's instructions. If you don't have a popcorn maker, heat the canola oil and popcorn kernels in a large pot over medium-high heat. Shake the pot from side to side occasionally until the first kernel pops. Cover with a lid and continue cooking, gently shaking the pot from side to side until the popping mostly subsides, about 2 minutes. Remove from the heat and take the lid off (any condensation on the lid will make the popcorn soggy). Drizzle the melted butter over the popcorn and season with salt. Pour into a serving bowl and set in the center of a large platter.

Arrange the licorice twists, chocolate candies, peanut butter cups, chocolate-covered honey grahams, and potato chips in bowls or directly on the platter to serve.

SERVES: 4
PREP TIME: 10 minutes
COOK TIME: 5 minutes

COOKIE BOARD

This board combines some of my favorite Trader Joe's cookies—soft snickerdoodles, crunchy meringues, and warm, gooey chocolate chip cookies fresh from the oven.

1 (16-ounce) package Trader Joe's Chunky Chocolate Chip Cookie Dough

1 (11.4-ounce) package Trader Joe's Maple Leaf Cookies

1 (7.76-ounce) package Trader Joe's Vanilla Meringues (gluten free)

1 (6-ounce) package Trader Joe's Soft Baked Snickerdoodles (gluten free)

1 (20-ounce) package Trader Joe's Joe-Joe's Chocolate Vanilla Creme Cookies (gluten-free option)

1 (8-ounce) package Trader Joe's Dark Chocolate Covered Honey Grahams with Sea Salt

VEGETARIAN, GLUTEN-FREE OPTIONS

Preheat the oven to 350°F. Line a baking sheet with parchment paper.

Bake the chocolate chip cookie dough for 10 to 12 minutes. Allow to cool for at least 10 minutes.

Arrange all the cookies on the board to serve.

SERVES: 4
PREP TIME: 10 minutes
COOK TIME: 10 to 12 minutes

Note: A few of the cookies on this list are naturally gluten-free, or TJ's offers a gluten-free equivalent. If serving someone who's on a gluten-free diet, make sure to keep them separated to avoid any cross-contamination.

FRUIT AND CHEESE DESSERT

I worked at a fine dining restaurant when I was in college, and a guest once asked me what was on our dessert cheese platter. I rushed to get the answer. The sous chef shouted the list of cheeses over the din of the kitchen. A week later, a review of the restaurant came out in the newspaper. Apparently, that guest was a food critic, and I had misheard. It wasn't "golden glow" as I had told him—an appetizing-sounding cheese, if you ask me. It was gorgonzola. My hot shame now a hilarious memory, I love cheese for dessert. And yes, I even include gorgonzola. This board follows the "holy trinity" of goat, cow, and sheep's milk cheeses. If you're not normally a fan of goat cheese, give TJ's Chevre with Honey a try. It's mild and sweet and pairs beautifully with the fruit.

1 (5-ounce) log Trader Joe's Chevre with Honey Goat's Milk Cheese

1 wedge roquefort or gorgonzola cheese

1 wedge Trader Joe's Saint André Triple Crème Brie

1 pint strawberries (ideally organic), some sliced and some left whole

1 pint blackberries

2 or 3 small clusters of red or green grapes

¼ cup dried cherries

VEGETARIAN, GLUTEN-FREE

Place the cheeses on the serving board.

Arrange the fresh fruit and dried cherries around the cheeses. Make sure the fruit is dry when you place it on the board so it won't make the cheeses soggy.

SERVES: 4
PREP TIME: 5 minutes

Note: Wondering how to pronounce chèvre? Start with the name of the American car company Chevrolet and leave off the last syllable—shev-ruh. This works well because the middle syllable of the car maker is unaccented, almost trailing off when you say the name of the cheese.

EPIC DESSERT BOARD

I had never realized exactly how many desserts are available at Trader Joe's until I went to create this board. I was overwhelmed by the options. I asked one of the guys in Hawaiian shirts to help, and he guided me to his top picks—more than a dozen sumptuous desserts that would have overflowed even my largest board and overwhelmed the appetites of four hungry teenagers. I created balance by offering a little something for everyone—crunchy cocoa batons, sweet macarons, buttery shortbread cookies, and creamy rich chocolate ganache cake. Gather all your friends and prepare to indulge your sweet tooth!

1 (18-ounce) package
Trader Joe's Dark Chocolate
Ganache Mini Sheet Cake

1 (16-ounce) package
Trader Joe's Dark Chocolate
Covered Almonds

1 (11-ounce) package
Trader Joe's Brownie +
Cookie = Brookie

1 (4.2-ounce) package Trader
Joe's A Dozen Macarons Variés

1 (5.29-ounce) package Trader
Joe's All Butter Shortbread
Sandwich Cookies

1 (8.47-ounce) package
Trader Joe's Blueberry
& Lemon Hand Pies

1 (5-ounce) package Trader
Joe's Cocoa Batons

VEGETARIAN

Slice the sheet cake into individual portions and place on the serving board. This can be messy, so while it's less fancy, you might consider leaving the cake pieces in the tray.

Pour the chocolate-covered almonds into a bowl and set it on the board, leaving a handful to sprinkle on the finished board.

Arrange the Brookie pieces on the opposite side of the board from the sheet cake. Place the remaining ingredients on the board, finishing with the cocoa batons and the reserved chocolate-covered almonds.

SERVES: 6 to 8
PREP TIME: 10 minutes

CHOCOLATE FONDUE

Fondue pots and fancy fondue forks are completely optional for this fun, social dessert board.

⅔ cup half-and-half

1 (10-ounce) package Trader Joe's 72% Cacao Dark Chocolate Chips

1 teaspoon vanilla extract

1 pound fresh strawberries

2 bananas, ripe but still firm

1 cup dried apricots

1 (3.6-ounce) package Trader Joe's Madeleine Cookies

VEGETARIAN, GLUTEN-FREE OPTION

Pour the half-and-half into a small saucepan and bring to almost a simmer over medium-low heat. Add the chocolate chips and stir until just melted. Stir in the vanilla. Remove from the heat, pour into a warmed bowl, and set in the center of the serving board.

Arrange the strawberries, bananas, apricots, and cookies around the bowl and serve immediately.

SERVES: 4
PREP TIME: 10 minutes
COOK TIME: 5 minutes

HOT COCOA BOARD

Normally I've avoided seasonal items in this book. But for this board I make an exception, because you're probably craving hot cocoa when snow (or rain) is falling and you see the following items on the shelves at your local TJ's. This hot cocoa board has only three essential ingredients—the rest is up to you to mix and match as you like. Have fun!

ESSENTIALS:

1 (10-envelope) box Trader Joe's Organic Hot Cocoa Mix

1 pint heavy cream or half-and-half

1 (10-ounce) package Trader Joe's Mini Marshmallows

OPTIONS:

1 (5-ounce) package Trader Joe's Cocoa Batons

1 (8-ounce) package Trader Joe's Dark Chocolate Covered Honey Grahams with Sea Salt

1 (16-ounce) package Trader Joe's Candy Cane Joe-Joe's

1 (8-ounce) tin Trader Joe's Peppermint Hot Chocolate

1 (10-ounce) package Trader Joe's Mini Dark Chocolate Mint Stars

1 (7-ounce) package Trader Joe's Chocolate Covered Sea Salt Butterscotch Caramels

VEGETARIAN, GLUTEN-FREE OPTION

Empty all the hot cocoa packets into a small bowl, add a spoon, and place on the board.

Pour the heavy cream or half-and-half into a small serving pitcher or a measuring cup and set on the board.

Add the marshmallows to the board, along with all the options you choose to use.

Bring a kettle of water to a boil, remove from heat, and pour into individual mugs for making cocoa.

SERVES: 8 to 10
PREP TIME: 10 minutes
COOK TIME: 2 minutes

Chapter 8

Extras

PICKLED VEGETABLES

Homemade pickled vegetables brighten any charcuterie board. My favorite vegetables to pickle are blanched green beans, carrots, red onions, and mini sweet peppers.

1½ cups white vinegar

1 cup water

2 tablespoons sea salt

2 tablespoons sugar

1 tablespoon coriander seeds

pinch red chili flakes

1 clove garlic, halved

2 to 4 cups raw vegetables, such as carrots, green beans, or mini sweet peppers, sliced

VEGAN, GLUTEN-FREE

Combine the vinegar and water in a small pot and bring to a simmer over medium heat. Add the sea salt and sugar and stir until dissolved. Remove from the heat.

Place the raw vegetables in a pint jar along with the coriander seeds, red chili flakes, and garlic. Pour in the brine to just cover the vegetables, then cover and refrigerate. If you can wait a day to enjoy these, please do. Otherwise, give them at least 4 hours to soak up the tangy, sweet, spicy brine before serving.

SERVES: 4
PREP TIME: 10 minutes
COOK TIME: 2 minutes

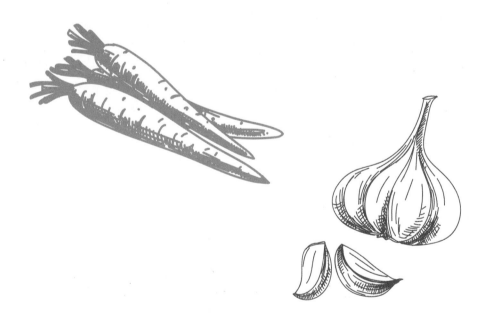

SPICED NUTS

Try not to polish off all these spiced nuts while you load them into a serving bowl—they're so addicting! These are amazing as an addition to a snack board or tossed in a salad.

¼ cup butter, melted

2 tablespoons brown sugar

2 teaspoons Trader Joe's Sriracha Sauce or other hot sauce (such as Cholula or Tapatio)

1 teaspoon sea salt

freshly ground black pepper

2 cups raw nuts (such as almonds, cashews, or pecans)

VEGETARIAN, GLUTEN-FREE

Preheat the oven to 350°F. Line a baking sheet with parchment paper.

In a large mixing bowl, combine the melted butter, brown sugar, hot sauce, salt, and pepper. Add the mixed nuts and toss to coat evenly with the spice mixture.

Spread the nuts in a single layer on the parchment-lined baking sheet. Bake for 10 to 12 minutes, stirring once or twice midway through.

Remove from the oven and let cool completely before serving.

SERVES: 4
PREP TIME: 10 minutes
COOK TIME: 10 to 12 minutes

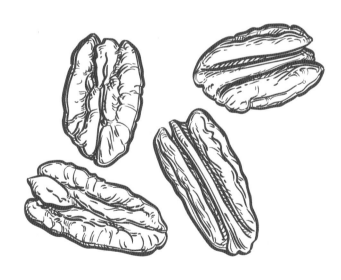

COMPOUND BUTTERS

These three compound butters elevate even the simplest ingredients. They're delicious on crusty bread or melted as a dip. You can also serve them over steak or steamed vegetables.

GARLIC AND HERB COMPOUND BUTTER

½ cup (1 stick) unsalted butter, softened

2 cloves garlic, minced

1 tablespoon chopped fresh parsley

1 tablespoon chopped fresh thyme

sea salt and freshly ground black pepper, to taste

VEGETARIAN, GLUTEN-FREE

In a medium mixing bowl, stir together the butter, garlic, parsley, and thyme with a spatula until well combined.

Season to taste with salt and freshly ground black pepper.

Transfer the garlic and herb butter to a lidded jar or other container and refrigerate until ready to use.

SUN-DRIED TOMATO AND BASIL COMPOUND BUTTER

½ cup (1 stick) unsalted butter, softened

¼ cup Trader Joe's California Sun-Dried Tomatoes, minced

2 tablespoons chopped fresh basil

sea salt and freshly ground black pepper, to taste

VEGETARIAN, GLUTEN-FREE

In a medium mixing bowl, stir together the softened butter, sun-dried tomatoes, and basil with a spatula until well combined.

Season to taste with salt and freshly ground black pepper.

Transfer the sun-dried tomato and basil butter to a lidded jar or other container and refrigerate until ready to use.

MAPLE PECAN COMPOUND BUTTER

½ cup (1 stick) unsalted butter, softened

¼ cup chopped toasted pecans

2 tablespoons Trader Joe's 100% Pure Maple Syrup

sea salt

VEGETARIAN, GLUTEN-FREE

In a medium mixing bowl, stir together the butter, pecans, and maple syrup with a spatula until well combined.

Season the mixture with a pinch of salt.

Transfer the maple pecan butter to a lidded jar or other container and refrigerate until ready to use.

YIELD: ½ cup
PREP TIME: 10 minutes

DIPPING OILS

While butter is a classic accompaniment to bread, dipping oils are a delicious and (some say) healthier alternative that can add a burst of flavor. These three dipping oils—herb, lemon pepper, and smoky chili—are easy to make and will elevate your bread game. Start with a good-quality extra-virgin olive oil—it really does make a difference!

LEMON PEPPER OIL:

½ cup extra-virgin olive oil

zest of 1 lemon

pinch sea salt

¼ teaspoon freshly ground black pepper

HERB OIL:

½ cup extra-virgin olive oil

¼ cup minced fresh herbs, such as rosemary, parsley, thyme, tarragon, and basil

pinch sea salt

SMOKY CHILI OIL:

½ cup extra-virgin olive oil

½ teaspoon red chili flakes

½ teaspoon smoked paprika

pinch sea salt

VEGAN, GLUTEN-FREE

Whisk together the ingredients for each oil in a separate container.

Allow the flavors to come together for at least 30 minutes before serving. The Smoky Chili Oil will keep, covered, for up to a month. The Lemon Pepper Oil and the Herb Oil should be used within a few days.

SERVES: 4
PREP TIME: 10 minutes

AIOLI

Aioli is a creamy and garlicky sauce that is a staple in Mediterranean cuisine. Enjoy it with Spanish Tortilla with Calabrian Chiles and Gremolata (page 56), crusty bread, grilled vegetables, or (in place of mayonnaise) Radishes with Kalamata Aioli (page 71).

2 egg yolks

¼ teaspoon Dijon mustard

1 clove garlic, finely minced using a Microplane grater

½ cup extra-virgin olive oil

1 tablespoon freshly squeezed lemon juice

salt and freshly ground black pepper, to taste

VEGETARIAN, GLUTEN-FREE

In a medium mixing bowl, whisk together the egg yolks, mustard, and minced garlic until well combined.

Gradually add the olive oil, whisking continuously until it has emulsified and the aioli starts to thicken. Add the lemon juice and continue whisking until the aioli reaches the desired consistency.

Season with salt and freshly ground black pepper to taste.

Transfer the aioli to a jar or other container, cover with a lid, and refrigerate until ready to use.

YIELD: ¾ cup
PREP TIME: 10 minutes

ESSENTIAL DIP

Every crudité board needs a good dip. While Trader Joe's has several ready-made options, if you want to create your own I recommend these three: Blue Cheese Dip, Fresh Herb Dip, and Spinach and Parmesan Dip. They all start with the same basic ingredients.

¼ cup mayonnaise

¾ cup sour cream

1 teaspoon lemon juice

1 small clove garlic, minced

sea salt

freshly ground black pepper

FOR BLUE CHEESE DIP:
4 ounces blue cheese, crumbled

FOR FRESH HERB DIP:
¼ cup minced fresh herbs, such as parsley, basil, and dill

2 tablespoons minced chives

FOR SPINACH AND PARMESAN DIP:
½ cup finely chopped cooked spinach

¼ cup grated parmesan cheese

VEGETARIAN, GLUTEN-FREE

Combine the mayonnaise, sour cream, lemon juice, and garlic in a small bowl. Season to taste with salt and pepper.

Stir in the additional ingredients listed for whichever dip you choose to make.

YIELD: 1 cup
PREP TIME: 10 minutes

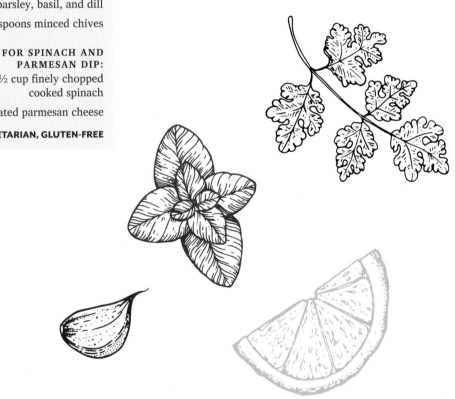

Recipe Index

References

Bon Appétit, "These 5 Cheese Plates Are Perfect, So Copy Them Exactly," www.bonappetit.com/story/cheese-plates-perfect; accessed 4/23/2023.

Smithsonian magazine, "Where Did the Taco Come From?" www.smithsonianmag.com/arts-culture/where-did-the-taco-come-from-81228162; accessed 4/29/2023.

CNBC, "A Trader Joe's Employee Reveals 4 Things You've Always Wanted to Know About the Store," www.cnbc.com/2019/04/04/4-things-you-always-wanted-to-know-about-trader-joes-from-an-employee.html; accessed 4/30/2023.

"The Strategy Story: Trader Joe's Business Model of 'Less is More,'" https://thestrategystory.com/2021/09/19/trader-joes-business-model; accessed 4/30/2023.

The New York Times, "Trader Joe's Defends Product Labels Criticized as Racist," www.nytimes.com/2020/08/01/us/trader-joes-jose-ming-joe-san.html; accessed 5/2/2023.

The Food Institute, "Simplicity Is Key to Trader Joe's Success," https://foodinstitute.com/focus/simplicity-is-key-to-trader-joes-success; accessed 5/2/2023.

Artwork Credits

page 14: blackberries © mamita

page 17: eggs © Net Vector

page 25: grapefruit © Alisa Pravotorova

page 26: bagels © AVA Bitter

page 35: gorgonzola © Genzi

page 36: grapes © Nikiparonak

page 39: antipasto © DiViArt

page 43: pita © mamba-hamba

page 44: bee, walnut, and olives © Epine

page 48: herbs © Epine

page 52: dates © Sabelskaya

page 63: bell peppers © B.illustrations

page 67: celery © Epine

page 71: radish © Epine

page 79: gyozas © valrylar

page 86: ketchup and mustard bottles © Epine

page 99: movie items © Bodor Tivadar

page 107: bananas © Epine; strawberries © ArtColibris

page 112: carrots and garlic © Natalya Levish

page 115: pecans © Nata_Alhontess

page 119: olive oil © Sketch Master

page 120: pepper grinder © Epine

page 123: lemon, garlic, and herbs © DiViArt

Conversions

MEASURE	EQUIVALENT	METRIC
1 teaspoon	--	5.0 milliliters
1 tablespoon	3 teaspoons	14.8 milliliters
1 cup	16 tablespoons	236.8 milliliters
1 pint	2 cups	473.6 milliliters
1 quart	4 cups	947.2 milliliters
1 liter	4 cups + 3½ tablespoons	1,000 milliliters
1 ounce (dry)	2 tablespoons	28.35 grams
1 pound	16 ounces	453.49 grams
2.21 pounds	35.3 ounces	1 kilogram
325°F/350°F/375°F	--	165°C/177°C/190°C

About the Author

Pamela Ellgen is the author of more than twenty cookbooks, including the best-selling *The 5-Ingredient College Cookbook*, *The Gluten-Free Cookbook for Families*, and *The Big Dairy Free Cookbook*. Her work has been featured in *Outside* magazine, *TODAY Food*, *Huffington Post*, *Darling Magazine*, and *The Portland Tribune*. When she's not in the kitchen, she's surfing with her two boys off the coast of San Diego. You can find her on Instagram @surfgirleats.